The Art of Parenting Together

How to Be Good Parents Together by Using Dynamic Parenting to Improve Your Kid's Childhood

Frank Dixon

Before we jump in, I'd like to express my gratitude. I know this mustn't be the first book you came across and yet you still decided to give it a read. There are numerous courses and guides you could have picked instead that promise to make you an ideal and well-rounded parent while raising your children to be the best they can be.

But for some reason, mine stood out from the rest and this makes me the happiest person on the planet right now. If you stick with it, I promise this will be a worthwhile read.

In the pages that follow, you're going to learn the best parenting skills so that your child can grow to become the best version of themselves and in doing so experience a meaningful understanding of what it means to be an effective parent.

Notable Quotes About Parenting

"Children Must Be Taught How To Think, Not What To Think."

– Margaret Mead

"It's easier to build strong children than to fix broken men [or women]."

- Frederick Douglass

"Truly great friends are hard to find, difficult to leave, and impossible to forget."

– George Randolf

"Nothing in life is to be feared, it is only to be understood. Now is the time to understand more, so that we may fear less."

– Scientist Marie Curie

Before we begin, I have something special waiting for you. An action-packed 1 page printout with a few quick & easy tips taken from this book that you can start using today to become a better parent right now!

It's my gift to you, free of cost. Think of it as my way of saying thank you to you for purchasing this book.

Claim your download of Profoundly Positive Parenting with Frank Dixon by scanning the QR code below and join my mailing list.

Sign up below to grab your free copy, print it out and hang it on the fridge!

Sign Up By Scanning The QR Code With Your Phone's Camera To Be Redirected To A Page To Enter Your Email And Receive INSTANT Access To Your Download

ARE YOU BUSY?

LISTEN TO THE AUDIOBOOK

ANYTIME. ANYWHERE.

EXCLUSIVELY AVAILABLE ON **audible**

Give Audible a try!

Sign up by scanning the QR code with your phone's camera

With Audible you can listen to this book and others like it

Regular offers include:

- Try Audible for $0.00
- Access a growing selection of included Audible Originals, audiobooks and podcasts.

Fully flexible:

- Email reminder before your trial ends.
- 30 day trial.
- Cancel anytime.

Table of Contents

INTRODUCTION **1**

CHAPTER 1: FAMILY DYNAMICS: THE CORE **5**

FAMILY TYPES AND THEIR IMPORTANCE 7

Factors That Affect Family Dynamics *11*

CHAPTER 2: WELL-FUNCTIONING AND DYSFUNCTIONAL FAMILIES **15**

WHAT DOES A HEALTHY FAMILY LOOK LIKE? 16

The Characteristics of a Dysfunctional Family *20*

CHAPTER 3: HEALTHY COMMUNICATION: A PIVOTAL ASPECT **27**

STYLES OF COMMUNICATION 30

Building an Unrestrained Environment *32*

CHAPTER 4: ACKNOWLEDGING PROBLEMS **37**

AN OVERVIEW OF COMMON PROBLEMS 38

Problem Resolution: Strategies That Work *41*

CHAPTER 5: BUILDING HEALTHY HABITS **45**

REPLACING A BAD HABIT WITH A POSITIVE ONE 47

Instilling a Positive Habit *49*

CHAPTER 6: ACTIVE LISTENING AND EMPATHY **53**

HOW ACTIVE LISTENING STRENGTHENS BONDS 54

Becoming an Active Listener *56*

CHAPTER 7: SCHEDULING QUALITY TIME TOGETHER **59**

BENEFITS OF FAMILY DOWNTIME 61

Family Activities Ideas for Downtime *62*

CONCLUSION 65

REFERENCES 67

Introduction

There are many people who have found themselves with great news but no one to share it with. Family, whether bound by blood, respect, or love, has a great significance in our lives. From our parents, mentors, and friends, there are some people who hold a special place in our hearts. People with strong support from their families have access to everyday joys. When hard times hit, they have people they can rely on. Family members are an immense source of encouragement, affection, and positivity in our lives. Even when we have a hard day at work, coming home to people whose eyes are filled with love and hope is enough to put us in a positive mood.

Family members are also mostly the first ones to detect signs of stress in us. They can notice the symptoms early on and show empathy. They can listen to, and provide, solutions. Family can bring a newer perspective to light—the one we often cannot see. In loving families, there is honesty, transparency, reciprocated love, and acceptance for one another. The love and warmth from the parents, unique bonds, and rivalry between siblings are all part of the package we call family.

There are many benefits of a healthy family life. For starters, it benefits the community. When families support each other financially, emotionally, and mentally, there is little pressure on the community to care for such people. Healthy families also raise children who make positive contributions toward the community. By helping the community, children often develop an attitude of caring. They engage in volunteering activities and help the people in their neighborhood, school, and other institutions succeed.

Children raised in a healthy family dynamic have a higher chance of attaining a healthy lifestyle. When meals are prepared with love and care, and when wisdom is put into opting for healthier alternatives to everyday junk foods, children develop healthy food choices. Their relationship with food improves. Various research confirms that children raised in a family setting live longer, eat healthier, and have active lifestyles. It is common knowledge that when reliance on junk and processed food becomes limited, there are fewer issues related to one's weight and physical health, as well.

Families also tend to one another's physical and emotional needs. From providing healthy food to good clothes and a comfortable shelter, parents look after their children's basic needs. But their role isn't confined to just food and shelter; they also support a child's emotional needs. If we look at Maslow's Hierarchy of Needs theory, we notice an emphasis on meeting emotional needs after physical needs. Emotional needs offer children protection and security. Daily positive interactions with the children can foster higher self-esteem and self-worth. Showing support for their dreams and passions shows children they are loved, validated, and wanted. Only when these emotional needs are met can one excel to the next level and reach the ultimate pinnacle—self-actualization.

Being raised in a family setting with loving parents and siblings also allows parents to instill good values and morals in children. In this hyper-connected world, we are surrounded by unhealthy ideas and exposed to fake news and obscene content. To ensure that children don't get involved in such vileness requires strong morals and ethics. They should have the power within to resist negativity and unhealthy influences. They should have the sense to choose better ideas and engage in constructive, skill-building, and wise activities. This is possible when children are shown a positive path to walk on. Strong family values prepare children and young ones to abstain from unwanted consequences or succumb to peer pressure. In family-oriented settings, parents can embody good values and empower children to make wise decisions.

Children need powerful role models when growing up. It is essential for their healthy development that they remain surrounded by people who are model citizens, resourceful parents, and great mentors. They can learn about kindness and positivity from their parents. They can follow in your footsteps if they feel guided along the way.

Besides that, growing children are bound to encounter social situations in their community and school. How they will face those situations depends on what they have been taught at home. Everything that a child learns or picks up is from the people around them. Patience, tolerance, kindness, and respect for others are examples of ideals they can pick up from their parents. These skills help them form meaningful relationships, hold friendly conversations, and navigate social situations self-reliantly.

If you are a parent or planning to start a family, good family dynamics are the most important way to strengthen family bonds. Giving your offspring a healthy environment to thrive in is a basic right. Good family dynamics allow children to enjoy positive relationships with everyone in their lives and keep the house an open, welcoming, and warm place.

Chapter 1:

Family Dynamics: The Core

Our families form an integral part of our lives. Those who are fortunate enough see their parents and siblings as the first few faces when starting their day. Despite the hectic lifestyles, a simple breakfast with the lot is enough to get everyone in a good mood. The dynamic a family shares becomes—the soul of every individual. Family dynamics are sets of interactions that happen. The relationship may not always be smooth, but the healthier it is, the stronger the family bonds are. Our family comprises the people we confide in, trust the most, and can't live without. Even in a love-hate relationship, it is difficult to remain isolated from the people we are bonded by blood with. The type of conversations we have, as well as interactions and connections, all form the backdrop of either a positive or negative family dynamic.

Family dynamics speak about a family's functioning. How they come together to resolve issues, deal with misfortunes, and hold each other in times of need determines the type of relationship there is. According to one study, strong family dynamics help families cope with stress better (Thomas et al., 2017). Family members feel supported and loved, despite the gravity of the situation they feel.

Conversely, families that don't share a healthy family dynamic can experience physical and mental stress. This is one reason therapists often question the patient about their family dynamics and upbringing during sessions. They want to know more about the experiences one had while growing up as they affect our actions, behaviors, and thought process.

In short, family dynamics are pervasive patterns of interaction that trickle down from one generation to another. They can be positive or unhealthy. Since they affect all areas of our growth and development, it is important that we understand how family dynamics work. This means that we need to see how connected we are to ourselves, how we develop insights, and how we understand conscious and unconscious choices we make. Realizing the type of family dynamics that one has in their house can help form positive relationships and experiences. It can help all family members become aware of their needs and can understand how their choices and decisions affect others.

Family Types and Their Importance

To further understand family dynamics, looking at the type of family can also help. As parents, we play a key role in setting the right dynamic. Think of a family as a TV show. Every member has a role to play. There is a measurement tool that determines who did well and who didn't. For example, in traditional households, fathers are responsible for earning bread for the family, whereas mothers are to raise children, look after them, and feed them. We expect them to keep the house clean and take care of everyone. Similarly, an elder sibling acts as an adult and secondary parent, guiding the younger sibling to develop good habits. These roles often overlap depending on the type of family. Let's learn the six important family types and what each type brings to the table in terms of healthy child upbringing.

Nuclear Family

The nuclear family is a traditional family structure. A nuclear family features two parents—a father and a mother—along with children. The children can be biological or adopted. The aim is to raise adults who are independent and confident through a joint effort. This means that both parents work together to raise a child as successful and happy as they can. The advantages of raising children in a nuclear family setting are financial stability, stable parenting, quality education, and health. Both parents take part in raising the child, and a strong emphasis is made on keeping communication channels open and supportive. The disadvantages include a lack of support from extended family and friends, which can lead to overworking and loneliness. It can also make conflict resolution harder when there is no intermediary to barge in and help the couple resolve their issues.

Single Parents

In the modern age, single-parent families are becoming more common. It isn't always a cause for worry about healthy child development. A single parent family features a single parent taking on the role of both parents. It can be a mother or a father, depending on what the circumstances are. The parent may be separated, divorced, unmarried, or widowed. The reasons for the separation may be unique, and therefore, they'll have a different effect on every child. The advantages of single-family households include sharing of chores with the kids; support from family and relatives; resilience and tolerance in children and the parent; and a stronger bond with the parent the child lives with. The disadvantages, however, can't be underestimated, either. There is often more financial burden on the parent, especially when the parent is a mother. Lack of or limitations of suitable job opportunities may mean little finances, which can make it difficult to look after the child in the best way possible. In case the parent wants to move on and start a new family, they remain worried about how their previous child will be treated in the new family.

Stepfamily

Many marriages end in divorce and separation. Although the parents might share child custody, some partners wish to remarry. The new family becomes the child's stepfamily. The child now has to blend in with the other children, which can be troublesome and stressful. They may experience anger, confusion, and frustration. They may feel neglected, unimportant, or invalidated. They may feel less loved and secondary. However, the situation isn't all bad. Many stepparents make excellent parents. They shower the child with love and care. They root for them to succeed and have all the best things in life. In a stepfamily setting, children have a big family to lean on for support. They still get to spend time with both their parents—although separately. They can form stronger bonds with both families and feel welcomed and loved. Speaking of the drawbacks, a child may need some time to adjust. They may have to witness fights between separated parents and expect to take sides. Children may feel unloved and become undisciplined.

Childless Family

Childless families comprise partners who choose not to have children or can't have them. One or both partners may feel like they aren't meant to be parents. We call this voluntary childlessness, and it is becoming more common in the current financially challenging times. Some partners wait to start a family, and by the time they feel they are in a good place financially, they can't have them. Those who opt to remain childless may do so because they have a booming career, want to enjoy life as partners, or travel extensively. According to a survey conducted by Pew Research Center, 44% of women in the childbearing ages reported being "unlikely or not too likely" to have children (Brown, 2021). Advantages include no dependency and reduced responsibility. It means no expenditure on baby products and food, which equals abundant income. It also means more time to go on adventures, travel, and more time to spend with one another. However, you can't deny that a house without a child's laughter may sometimes cause sadness. One partner may feel like they are missing something important in their lives if they are fond of children.

Extended Family

Extended family features two or more people bound by either marriage or blood. Children brought up by extended family live in the same house as their aunts, uncles, or grandparents. Extended families often take over when both parents are unavailable because of challenging work commitments, a divorce, or are deceased. Growing up, the child might feel isolated, unloved, and ignored. Although extended families do offer the same warmth and comfort, sometimes, they can't replace a parent. Benefits of living in an extended family include 24/7 support in case of emergencies; mental and social support; and division of chores. But you can also expect to complain about a lack of privacy, interference in your personal matters, and financial instability in case there is just one income and more stomachs to feed.

Grandparent Families

Although uncommon, this is also an important family structure type where grandparents of the child become the guardians. They raise children because the parents are unavailable or get embroiled in severe circumstances. For example, an arrest or medical treatment can be two reasons. To avoid them from ending up in foster care, grandparents take the custody of the child/children and raise them as their own. There is a significant change in this parenting style as there is a big age gap. Grandparents may not be accustomed to the needs and well-being of a child growing up in a unique setting. As they are also seniors, they may not be as active and well-equipped to care for a young one and tend to all its basic needs. But there are also some advantages, too. Living with grandparents can help children develop good habits and morals. They can be raised with affection and care as opposed to being left under foster care. Children can also remain in touch with the extended family and enjoy life with blood cousins their age.

Factors That Affect Family Dynamics

Different factors also contribute to the type of dynamic there is in the family. The art of parenting involves working together as a team since the goal is the same: a healthy family dynamic. Since every individual brings something unique to the mix, below are some factors that can define family dynamics.

For starters, the relationship between the parents, whether living together or separated, sets the mood of the house. If the relationship is positive, it will garner positive vibes. If the relationship is bitter, the dynamic in the house will be unpleasant as well. If one or both parents are strict or soft, the experiences will be different as well. In a strict and disciplined household, children see their parents as their guardians and mentors. They respect them like they would respect an adult. There is little room for silliness because discipline is taught. In homes where parents act as their child's friend and an authority figure, the environment will be more relaxed. There will be more room to have difficult conversations, more transparency, and more honesty between the parent and child.

How many children one has also defines family dynamics. The personality of family members also impacts the air in the house.

If one or both parents are absent, it can also affect the family dynamic since roles will then be nontraditional and circumstantial.

In many cultures, it is a common sight to have a mix of families live together. In such joint-family households, there is a different hierarchical order that prevails. It predetermines the roles everyone has to play, and therefore, a complex dynamic may exist. As extended families share a single roof, children are brought up in different influences from all members and not just the parents or siblings. They may feel closer to their cousins or grandparents rather than their siblings or parents.

Family structure and atmosphere also change when parents have to care for a sick or disabled child in the family. They provide more attention and care to the sick or handicapped child, leaving other children feeling left out or unimportant. You can imagine a not-so-pleasant family dynamic then.

Family dynamics can also change when the family goes through a crisis. It can be an affair leading to separation between parents, trauma, death, homelessness, or unemployment. In case of unemployment, one parent might have to take a second job, leaving them with little time to invest in their family. It also puts more pressure on the spouse that's left without a job, as they have to take on more responsibilities around the house and kids.

Sadly, these aren't the only issues that affect family dynamics. In some homes, cases of violence, abuse, drug use, disability, alcohol, and mental health difficulties also influence the nature of upbringing a child receives.

Family dynamics are also influenced by culture, beliefs, ethnicity, gender, parenting practices, and socioeconomic systems. Different parenting styles, as well as traditions and cultures, can impact how parents spend time with their children. The type of attachment they have with their offspring (secure vs. insecure) can also lead to unique child development.

Chapter 2:

Well-Functioning and Dysfunctional Families

As parents, we often wonder what an ideal family looks like. Is it similar to what we see in ads where actors always have the biggest smiles on their faces, and their days are spent painting walls, assembling furniture, or having backyard movie nights? We see parents and children cooking together, playing together, and tending to each other's needs.

Then we look at our family dynamic and wonder if we are doing enough or not. However, just because you aren't always running after your kids, having pillow fights with them on a Sunday morning, or going on a trip together with your pet dog doesn't mean your family dynamic isn't healthy.

A healthy family dynamic is an environment where everyone feels loved, respected, and appreciated—regardless of the time they spend together. Even if your children keep to themselves and prefer to stay in their rooms than spend time with you, you can still ensure a healthy and friendly dynamic. As long as they know they can come to you with their problems and you will hear them out, it's healthy.

A well-functioning family doesn't have to stick together to express love and affection. They can express it in various forms such as being an active listener, setting healthy boundaries, and respecting each other's opinions and ideas.

In this chapter, we look at the differences between a well-functioning and dysfunctional family to learn more about healthy family dynamics and how you can achieve one in your home.

What Does a Healthy Family Look Like?

A strong and healthy family, according to research, has a wide range of qualities that add to its well-being (DeFrain & Asay, 2007). The research reviewed the lives of people from different races, social and economic groups, as well as different family settings across the globe and found that even the strongest of families have problems. It redefines the model of a functional family and states that it isn't the opposite of a dysfunctional family. Researchers talked about how there were many common variants and challenges that every family has to cope with, such as everyday life stresses as well as larger traumas like someone's death.

Well-functioning families are better equipped to deal with the challenges they come across than dysfunctional families.

Apart from this, there are some characteristics that distinguish a well-functioning family from a dysfunctional one. In well-functioning families, love, respect, and a sense of belongingness reigns supreme. Every member of the family feels welcomed to give their input. The communication lines are open, and opinions are respected. The goal is to make sure that every member feels equally respected, valued, and esteemed.

To determine whether your family is a functioning one or dysfunctional, ask yourself the following questions.

- Does humor find a place in the house despite the real demands of everyday life?
- Are their clear rules in the house? How are they applied? Is there room for some flexibility?
- How does the family respond to new situations and changes?
- Does the family have reasonable expectations of each other? Are they mutually agreed upon and fulfilled?
- Do family members feel like their needs are met or not?

- Do they achieve most of their set goals and dreams?
- Is there respect between parents and children?
- Do parents and children feel comfortable in demonstrating love, care, and concern?
- How are disagreements handled? Does every member get to have a say or are all decisions taken by the authority figure?

In short, these are the most distinguishable qualities of a well-functioning family, whether governed by a single parent or a married couple.

Commitment: There is loyalty among family members. They share responsibilities, get everyone involved in the decision-making process, and support each other in important life decisions.

Appreciation and Affection: There is affection toward all family members. They keep promises they make to one another. They appreciate each other's contribution in the household and are genuine in their praise.

Effective Communication: Healthy communication forms the essence of a well-functioning family. There is free expression of ideas, emotions, and thoughts. There is listening without judgment or criticism. Members of a well-functioning family don't interrupt or argue with each other. They resolve conflicts with utmost respect without putting each other down.

Excellent Coping Skills: Well-functioning families are more resilient since they go through arduous experiences as a team. A crisis brings them closer. They form each other's backs when there is need and are eager to help each other come out of a critical situation.

Acceptance: Every member of a well-functioning family accepts each other as they are. They accept people who can be different. The differences can be of intelligence, talent, personality, success at school, or beliefs. It is acceptance that allows all family members to prosper in their personal and professional lives.

Emotional Encouragement: Well-functioning families encourage the expression of emotions. They share happy, sad, exciting, and tender moments together. They acknowledge one's anger and frustration and help cope with it. They do so by gently probing, showing empathy, and validating one's emotions and feelings—even when they don't understand them.

Damage Repair Skills: Finally, healthy and well-functioning families do damage repair. If there is a conflict, all members do their best to resolve it and mend relationships. They understand that conflict is a part of one's life, and if issues linger for long, they can promote negative feelings. Therefore, to avoid relational distance, they put their emotions aside and reach a compromise where everyone is happy.

All these qualities are connected and often overlap each other. They help families stick together and remain glued with one another in a pleasant and friendly manner.

The Characteristics of a Dysfunctional Family

In *Anna Karenina*, Leo Tolstoy (1878), the Russian novelist, writes that all happy families are the same, but all unhappy families are unhappy in their own way. We know what a well-functioning family looks like. We know how communication is of importance to them and how respect is viewed, discipline is practiced, and acceptance for all is the motto. They too have some problems, but they aren't emotionally dysfunctional.

Just because a family is run by a single parent—two parents who are separated, divorced, or remarried into new families—doesn't mean that the family will be dysfunctional. Even a nuclear family can have the features of a dysfunctional family because parents don't work together to raise happy and successful children.

When we use the term "dysfunctional," we refer to households and families where neglect toward children is a common issue. There is secrecy, addiction, and sometimes abuse. When these issues are brought to light, the family denies their influence. However, when a child's emotional and mental well-being comes into question, we need to rethink the type of environment and structure we are providing them. For this, we need to discuss the unique but negative traits that are common in all dysfunctional families. Learning about these qualities will help us avoid adopting them and becoming a dysfunctional family.

Most dysfunctional families have a pattern of negative behaviors. Dysfunctional behavior also refers to disorganization. It means that one puts in the least amount of effort or is deliberately sloppy and neglectful. For example, a parent not tending to the needs of a sick child is neglectful on purpose. Such unhealthy elements lead to resentments and challenging times for the family. It becomes even more problematic when there is physical, sexual, or emotional abuse. Destructive family systems are abusive or emotionally neglectful. Abuse is sometimes directed at the spouse and other times, toward the child. It can include cases of domestic violence and sexual assault like molesting a child. Emotional abuse also comes under the same criteria because it equally harms the individual. Emotional abuse and trauma may take longer to heal as opposed to any physical injury. Some children and spouses never overcome the trauma and have to live with it all their lives.

Neglecting a child's basic needs, like providing food, shelter, or clothing, are also features of a dysfunctional family. Parents don't take care of an infant's basic needs like changing a dirty diaper for hours, not giving the child a bath, or letting the child cry before feeding them. As little ones can't take care of themselves or be vocal about their needs, this is the worst kind of neglect and abuse one can imagine.

In a dysfunctional household, there is also fear and unpredictability. There is little trust between family members. Constant fear of being mistreated, disrespected, or left behind keeps lurking. A child fears their parent's reaction. They fear they will be scolded, beaten, or grounded for sharing a desire or expressing their honest opinions about something. A spouse may feel like their efforts go unappreciated. They may also feel like they are criticized over every little thing that they do with so much heart.

Second, dysfunctional families avoid things labeled as enjoyable. They won't opt for planning a vacation or holiday as a family. They know that in doing so, they will have to spend time together and act as a team. When abuse and neglect is involved, problems and arguments are bound to arise. If both partners are short-tempered, it becomes impossible to go on a trip together and enjoy it. It becomes a game of comebacks where both partners keep passing harsh and hurtful comments to each other.

Another thing that's prevalent in dysfunctional families is addiction. Excess of anything is termed as dangerous. Spouses that engage in substance abuse may become neglectful of their children, as the feeling of being "high" becomes a priority. Similarly, if one or both spouses are heavy drinkers, they may not be in a fit state to take care of children. If they are into drugs or any other form of addiction, like gambling or watching porn, it can only make matters worse for everyone in the house.

Another feature that stands out in dysfunctional families is the lack of boundaries. Lack of healthy boundaries can mean different things. It can involve a controlling parent that doesn't consider the opinions of others. They act as an authority figure and decide for everyone in the house. This can lead to children feeling invalidated and unimportant. Lack of boundaries can also mean an intimidating parent. An intimidating parent is one that actively discourages, scares, or asserts themselves on others. They believe others are always in the wrong and what they think is right. An intimidating parent can prevent a child from reaching their full potential, as many learning and excelling opportunities go unanswered.

Lack of boundaries can also mean no privacy or personal space. Everyone tries to do things their way and pry in the matters of others. There is no respect for the ideas of others.

In many dysfunctional families, there is almost no understanding between family members. Whenever someone tries to speak their mind and put forth an idea or suggestion, they are met with conflict, ridicule, and criticism. There are mixed messages that create confusion and an unhealthy environment to reach a common consensus. When children fear being rejected, there remains a sense of tension in the house. This isn't appropriate for young children to witness, as they are quick to pick up on the behaviors and attitudes of their parents and older siblings. In dysfunctional homes, family members don't feel safe communicating with those who claim authority. Issues are swept under the rug instead of being resolved. There is no concept of apology or remorse, as everyone thinks they are in the right. This proves that there are no open lines for effective communication to take place.

In a dysfunctional setting, there is a lack of compassion and emotional intimacy as well. Healthy patterns of attention and love aren't practiced. There is little closeness among family members because no one trusts the other or others. Showing care and affection may be withheld when the goal is to punish a child. Some parents also show a lack of compassion toward their children or treat them unequally. For example, one child receives love from their parents while the other remains wanting.

Finally, there is rigid perfectionism as well. Dysfunctional families don't set realistic expectations. They are too high or too low, causing a rift between relationships. If expectations are too high, the child keeps failing to meet them. If they are too low, the child feels like the parents think too poorly of them. Perfectionism can never be achieved, as we come across unique situations every other day. With unrealistic expectations, parents set children up for failure, which nurtures resentment and anger in them. Often, comparisons are also made with cousins or a friend's children. This can further eat up a child's self-confidence and worth. They may start to believe that their actions, no matter how perfect and thoughtful, will never garner the same appreciation as the children of others. This takes away the motivation to prove everyone wrong.

Expecting a child to be perfect puts a lot of pressure on them. They constantly feel like they have to prove themselves worthy of the love and attention they receive. If they cannot meet the set goals, it affects their emotional and mental health as well.

Chapter 3:

Healthy Communication: A Pivotal Aspect

Many families, living together or separated, fail to improve family relationships and interactions because they don't understand the complex role communication plays. When communication isn't open or up to par with what it needs to be, disagreements and conflicts arise. Emotions go unheard and get brushed under the rug. No compromises are reached, and this prevents the facilitation of real change.

If you feel like your family could do better with improved communication lines and openness, know that it can be an easy fix. At first, it may feel awkward to initiate and discuss things together, but in the near future, it will become an instrumental tool to improve family dynamics, especially when two parents are co-parenting a child but not living together. With some tact and perseverance, engaging in healthy conversations isn't difficult for families.

Healthy family communication refers to both verbal and nonverbal exchange of ideas and information. To communicate, you have to hear as well as you speak. Additionally, you have to pay attention to what the individual isn't vocal about such as their feelings, body language, and facial expressions.

Effective communication has to take place to enable all family members to share their needs, concerns, and desires. Being honest and open to new perspectives and ideas is a positive feeling. When you know how your actions and words affect others, you can model your conversations better. You can keep in mind the sensitive nature of others and be more empathetic. This is also important when you have more than one child in the house with different personalities. Some will be more sensitive than others, and knowing the right way to communicate will strengthen the bond.

Open communication among family members creates an atmosphere that allows family members to express their opinions, admiration, and differences for one another. Open communication lines can prevent lingering issues that arise. By being honest about how one feels, conflicts can be resolved in less time.

In some homes, communication happens, but it isn't the right pattern. Unhealthy communication patterns can also prevent individuals from expressing their needs openly. You must be aware of these patterns. For example, it can be aggressive when parents or children use threats, criticisms, and other demeaning strategies to get their wishes fulfilled. Being aggressive is a toxic trait, and if any of the parents embody it, chances are that the children will be afraid of them. Aggressive family members hold immense power and authority within the family. Others don't want to bother or involve them in their matters, as they are aware that things will become heated. Children, in particular, wish to avoid engaging with them, as they fear landing themselves in trouble.

Second, communication may also be passive-aggressive. An example of a passive-aggressive act is telling someone that you are fine when you are not. Acting this way toward children can make them feel upset or confused. It's like saying one thing and meaning another. Expectations become confusing for children, as they don't know what to do and what not to do. Even when they know that you are lying to them, you keep assuring them that you are not, which can make them feel disrespected and frustrated.

Communication can also be passive where one family member subdues their needs for the sake of others. Passive communicators are people-pleasers. Their actions and words are directed toward another person's happiness. They put others before them and willingly sacrifice having any opinions themselves. At first, this might seem like a positive trait, but when you live with a passive communicator, it can quickly become annoying. Family members secretly wish that passive communicators would have an opinion of their own and take an active part in decision-making. Their dependence on others makes them lose respect in the eyes of other family members.

Finally, giving the silent treatment to family members is also an unhealthy communication pattern. Here, a family member cuts off all communication ties and shuts down emotionally. This is most common during a conflict or argument. This silent treatment can make the other person feel helpless and angry, as conflicts remain unresolved. This silent treatment toward the individual may last for a few hours or days. It can bring resentment and annoyance in relationships.

Styles of Communication

Communication and families have a symbiotic relationship. Family communication encompasses how family members interact with one another. It talks about the type of relationship there is between parents, children, and siblings. Together, they create a unique family dynamic that makes families distinguishable from one another. Proper communication patterns reflect and construct a family's reality.

Apart from different patterns, communication can also have different areas and styles. It can be instrumental or effective. Instrumental communication involves the exchange of factual information between individuals. This allows for the fulfillment of common family functions. For instance, telling a child to clean their room after playing is an instrumental communication exchange. You are telling them to put their toys back in their place so that they can find them easily the next day. Affective communication is an exchange between family members where they share their emotions. For instance, your child may come up to you when they feel sad for being scolded at school. The exchange of communication involves showing empathy, support, and care, making your child feel less stressed.

In 1993, a group of researchers studied the complex model of family assessment and treatment and its relationship with communication. The findings were later published in 2000 and listed four styles of communication that happen within a family (Miller et al., 2000).

It can be clear and direct. Being clear and direct is the healthiest form of communication, as the message remains plain and easily understandable for all. It prevents confusion and sets clear expectations. For example, a mother may tell her son that she feels disappointed because he didn't take out the trash despite being told to. That is clear and direct communication, as the son knows the reason for his mother's disappointment, and the mother has the chance to express her displeasure.

The second style of communication is clear but indirect. Here, the message gets distorted because communication isn't direct. The message is clear, but it isn't intended toward the right family member. For example, a mother may show displeasure when she sees the trash can full of trash but not say who she is disappointed at. She may be vague in her displeasure and say something like, "I am disappointed when people forget their chores." The son who forgot to take out the trash may not decipher the intended message that was for him.

The third style of communication is masked and direct communication. In this style, the message becomes vague or unclear but is directed at the right family member. For example, the mother may tell her son that she hates it when people don't work as hard as they used to. Here, the son knows that he did something wrong. However, what he did wrong remains unclear or masked.

The fourth style of communication is masked and indirect. This happens when both the message and the intended recipient aren't clear. This is common in dysfunctional families because there is no openness. If we look at the same example, the mother might say something like this, "The youth of today is good for nothing." Here, neither the message nor the recipient is clear. This can confuse and cause resentment as more than one person in the family will get offended, thinking the criticism is directed toward them.

Building an Unrestrained Environment

To improve communication in the household, we must, therefore, create an unrestrained environment where everyone feels free to express their ideas, opinions, and feelings. It is through communication that family members can define their identities and negotiate their relationships. Communication in the house is what prepares us to connect with the rest of the world through appropriate dialogue and social skills. If you look closely at your family, you will notice how communication differentiates your family members from nonfamily members. There is an invisible barrier that you don't cross when speaking with others, but it's different when you are surrounded by your family members. For a child, it is the same. They find it easier to share their thoughts with their family members than with their relatives or teachers. It just comes naturally to them.

Given the increasing complexities of family forms such as family bonds by remarriage, single parenting, chosen partnerships, etc., communication patterns have changed as well. They mold the family dynamics differently. Researchers have found a strong link between these communication patterns and marital satisfaction in relationships (Noller & Fitzpatrick, 1990). According to one study, the more positively a couple rated their communication, the more satisfied they seemed with their relationship (Markman, 1981). The relationships were followed up by the researchers after five years, and they found that effective communication did play a key role in setting the family dynamic.

So, how can you improve communication among family members, especially between a parent and child? Below are some ideas.

Be Available: That is the first and most important rule. You have to be present for your children. In today's world, lack of proper time is regarded as a greater problem than financial crisis (Duxbury et al., 2018). Schedule some free time from your busy lives for your children every day and have a one-on-one conversation with them. It doesn't have to be about anything specific. You can ask about a movie they watched the other day, their day at school, or how their friends are. Even sectioning out 10 minutes for them without distractions will make a huge difference in your child's life and improve communication between you two.

Show Appreciation Whenever You Can and Be Quick with Your Feedback: Children love being commended. Timely feedback prompts positive action and increases its likelihood in the future. You can offer praise whenever you catch them doing something constructive. This requires a vigilant eye and intention. The praise should also sound genuine and well-directed, meaning the child should know what action garnered the positive response.

Make Communications Clear and Direct: Be clear about what you expect from your spouse and children. Don't play the blame game and use criticism as a means to counter arguments. Keep your message clear and well-intended. Take into consideration the emotions and nature of others as well to avoid hurting them unintentionally. Indirect or vague arguments will further create problems and contribute to a lack of emotional bonding and intimacy between family members.

Model Good Behaviors as Children Learn Through You: Be careful of not just the words that you use in the house but also your tone. The way you speak to your child or spouse is the way they are going to speak to you and others. Ensure that your tone of voice gets the message across calmly and genuinely.

Be Empathetic: Children have feelings, too, and words can be the sharpest weapon against them. When your child comes to you for support and guidance, ensure that they feel supported and loved. A simple hug or pat on the back is enough to encourage positivity along with a few supportive words. Let them know that you understand what they are going through, and you wish you could help them feel better. Just the validation of it will gradually uplift their mood because they feel less lonely.

Chapter 4:

Acknowledging Problems

Many problems and arguments arise in a family. Most issues arise because of different parenting styles and how parents wish to raise their children. As the children grow a little older, what schools to enroll them in, what extracurricular activities to allow them to engage in, and how to teach them chores in the house all become common points for arguments between spouses.

You might have also fought with your spouse or child over something at some point. The specifics of the conflict may be different, but there is a strategic way to resolve conflicts. It starts with the acknowledgment of a problem. In many homes, when a parent finds out that their teenage child has been taking drugs or consuming alcohol, the first thing they do is punish the child. They don't view the reasoning as a problem behind drinking or drug abuse. They only discipline them. Acknowledging why the child started to take drugs in the first place, finding out the root cause that triggers the need every time, and what influences surround them are the key factors to take into consideration. Rewarding or punishing the act isn't enough. Knowing the root cause is.

Even well-functioning families come across situations that they think are out of their control. If they don't acknowledge the core issue at hand and keep beating around the bush instead, they too will fail at responding to it appropriately.

Therefore, in this next chapter, we take a look at some of the most common problems, as listed by many family counselors, that ruin a healthy family dynamic as well as the best ways to counter them to raise happy and emotionally healthy children.

An Overview of Common Problems

As stated above, problem identification and acknowledgment is the first step to creating positive change. Commonly, when parents are questioned about the biggest hurdles and challenges they face with children, they list the following behavioral issues:

Back Talking

Back talking is common with toddlers as well as teenagers. They want to question their parent's methods and directions. This happens when there is a need for independence. They want to take control of their lives, but their knowledge about the world and how it functions is limited. Thus, there arises a conflict of interest in which both parties argue and talk back.

Ignoring Instructions

This is similar to back talking. Here, the child deliberately ignores what they have been told to do or say and does the opposite. This can also create a rift between the parent and the child because they have to reestablish their authority. Ignoring instructions or not listening to them on purpose is a behavior acquainted with children of all ages.

Throwing Temper Tantrums

Children throw tantrums when their request is refused by a parent. They have a meltdown that involves crying, screaming, and at times, throwing things or laying on the ground and rubbing their knees against it. A tantrum can be hard to stop once it begins. The best way is to prevent one.

Disobedience

Misbehaving with parents and other adults like relatives or teachers is another common issue with toddlers. They don't like to be told what to do. Disobedience can test a parent's patience, as the message they are trying to preach doesn't get across. It can even cause an argument over the style of parenting between parents, as one wants to practice strict disciplining strategies while the other wants to keep things friendly.

Picky Eaters

Children have a distinct sense of what textures, aromas, and flavors they like. They aren't comfortable with change, and therefore, they will cause a ruckus every time you present them with something new. Picky eaters can throw temper tantrums when forced to try something new for a change or when not presented with what they wanted.

Sibling Rivalry

Sibling rivalry is a real and unavoidable issue in most homes. Some children feel that their sibling is loved and appreciated more, so they start to dislike them. They don't want to play or share things with, and whenever they are requested to share, they start to fight.

Parenting Styles

Different upbringings and family cultures can cause disagreements between parents, as they want to raise them with values and beliefs close to them. This usually starts with whether or not to have kids or when to have them. Then comes fights about disciplinary training, religions, schooling, and many other things such as how much freedom to allow the child. Disagreements are fine as long as parents are ready to sit down and find a solution together.

Poor Communication

Miscommunication or a lack of communication, in general, can also lead to the arising of issues in the family. Miscommunication leads to a lot of things going wrong because things get interpreted wrong or remain unsaid. Any relationship that doesn't encourage openness, acceptance, and honesty has a poor survival rate.

Difficult Family Members

Some family members require more attention and care than others. It could be due to a medical condition or sensitive nature. This can cause other family members to feel left out or ignored. Sometimes, additional attention and care can stress out a parent because they fail to fare well in their other responsibilities like work and household chores. They are also left with little or no time for self-care practices which can further induce fatigue and stress.

Problem Resolution: Strategies That Work

The second step after acknowledgment of a problem is finding its solution. You need to think about what changes you need to make to prevent a meltdown, temper tantrum, and attention-starved children. You need to find a middle ground where children are given autonomy as well as taught about discipline. You need to work on improving communication so that your message sounds genuine, clear, and full of empathy.

Start with one problem at a time. It can be a challenging behavior, such as your child being a picky eater. If you want to change this behavior, start by noticing what triggers it. Jot down the things that your child loves to eat and also the ones they are reluctant to eat. Next, generate ideas on how you can incorporate healthy ingredients by blending them with the foods they like. For example, if your child finds eating a carrot too hard to chew, slice it in thin, julienne style and add it to a salad they like to eat. You can also boil and blend it with other vegetables like potatoes and make fries or potato cutlets. If this doesn't work and the child still avoids eating it, move on to another idea that you think will work better. Gradually test different ideas out and see what works best for you. Notice their reactions and resolve other problems the same way. First, identify the trigger, come up with a set of ideas, and pick the one that works best.

Secondly, if you want to discipline the child over a bad habit or behavior, make sure that the child knows it is the behavior that is the problem and not the child. Many parents fail to distinguish between the two and end up scolding their children. There are hundreds of reasons why a child resorts to a certain behavior. It isn't always to cause trouble. They may want more time or attention from you. Besides, scolding the child might cause further stress. A child may get more engaged and stubborn.

Express your feelings and emotions. Sometimes, we assume that the other person will take the hint and read our minds. We believe that they will know what we want or need. In most cases, a parent knows what the child wants, but what about those other times when they don't? You'll want to build an atmosphere in the house where everyone feels comfortable speaking their mind. Self-expression can prevent disappointments and negative behaviors. It also improves family dynamics in the house.

Try using more "I" statements. When trying to resolve an argument or problem, statements starting with "You" puts the other person at blame. They feel they are being accused. Using statements starting with "I" takes away guilt and blame.

Finally, pick your battles wisely. Not every action demands a reaction. Do you want to be right or happy? This is an important question to ask yourself. Throwing stones over every negative behavior will lead to more problems than solutions. Furthermore, address the problem rather than playing the blame game. That would only mean you want to be right.

Chapter 5:

Building Healthy Habits

Bad habits interrupt life. Habits like procrastination; poor eating and sleeping schedules; and lack of focus and physical activity prevent us from accomplishing our goals. They also jeopardize mental and physical health.

We often wonder how bad habits are formed. They are either the result of boredom or stress. Stress can make us bite our nails and do stupid or risky things. Boredom can lead to binge eating, wasting precious time, and procrastinating on what's important. When we remain distracted or deliberately put off with what's important, we end up with more stress. People who drink do so to forget their sorrows and worries. People who go on a shopping spree do it because they have nothing else to do. Children who spend hours playing video games or making snaps on social media sites do it because they are bored, too.

But should it be this way? Why can't we give up on negative behaviors and teach ourselves to adopt new and healthy habits? How hard can it be?

It's especially hard when we don't address the reasons that trigger those habits and behaviors. As parents, we are quick to point out a negative behavior we see our offspring engaged in. We respond with criticism without addressing the real cause. We need to go deeper and think about how a certain behavior develops into a habit and why.

Recognizing the cause behind those actions is the first step to eliminating them.

Good habits don't just happen. We introduce ourselves to them. Then, with self-discipline and patience, we incorporate them into our daily routines until we no longer have to be reminded to do them. They come naturally to us.

Take brushing our teeth, for instance. When we were younger, our parents instilled the habit of brushing our teeth daily. They repeated the instructions on how to brush properly every night until we got it right. They told us how brushing daily would benefit our gums and keep our teeth healthy and white. On days that we forgot to brush, they reminded us and instructed us to do it. The repeated instructions and practice turned into a habit. Today, as we step into the restroom in the morning, brushing our teeth is a natural urge. When we reach the sink, our hands instantly go for the toothbrush and toothpaste.

Replacing a Bad Habit With a Positive One

Habits, good or bad, are there for a reason. They take their sweet time to become one and therefore need as much time to be eliminated. In many cases, our habits benefit us in positive and negative ways. For example, the benefit may be biological. Not smoking keeps your lungs and liver healthy. Smoking does the opposite. It takes away years from your life. Similarly, good habits, like sleeping on time, yield positive benefits like giving your body and mind ample time to relax and recharge. You can feel more energized upon waking up. You can focus better and finish every task with efficiency.

In many ways, a bad habit is a coping mechanism. For example, tapping your foot, pacing forth and back, and clenching your fists when anxious allows you to become distracted. It helps you forget your worries for a while, and that is why every individual that practices the habit sticks to it.

Since these habits offer momentary rewards and an escape, we can't make the mind eliminate them from scratch. It's easy to tell someone to lose weight but difficult to do it. It is easy to tell someone to stop binge eating but hard to do it. What we must advise others is to replace the old habit with a newer, positive one. A habit that offers similar benefits is an excellent alternative. For example, if the reason someone drinks is to ease their nerves and calm their mind, they should look for alternate ways that promise similar rewards but are positive. For example, instead of drinking, one can watch a comedy sketch, listen to some soft tunes, or talk to someone they love.

The goal is to abstain from bad habits and engage in positive ones while addressing the reasons that serve as triggers. Cutting out bad habits without addressing the root cause will increase stress. Your needs will remain unmet. This will make it harder for you to stick to positive habits in the long run.

The first thing you need to do is, therefore, identify the trigger. An urge to light a cigarette may increase when your colleagues are having one too. it may also increase when you are sitting idle with your thoughts. Therefore, find alternative ways to counter this urge. You may choose to go for a walk when your colleagues go for a smoke break in the corridor. You may create a list of chores that you must complete before the end of the day so that you rarely find yourself with any free time.

You can also find a substitute habit to replace a bad one. This would require planning ahead of time so that you don't end up with a triggering situation, individual, or place. For the heavy drinker, a bar isn't the most ideal place to be, as they are surrounded by drinks and other drinkers. Think of the things you can do in case you feel triggered. What are you going to do when someone offers you a drink? How are you going to respond? How are you going to avoid drinking when your friends encourage you to have just one? You need to think about such possible scenarios and have a plan of action.

Next, you must surround yourself with people who live the way you aspire to live. It can be a role model, your parents, or a visionary you want to be like. This doesn't mean that you cut ties with people you know. You simply need to limit your interactions with them, as they trigger a bad habit, and spend more time with the ones that practice good habits. For example, if you want to calm your nerves and become mindful, you can join a yoga class and make new friends there.

Instilling a Positive Habit

Building a positive habit takes time. An action must be repeated again and again to train the brain into doing it. However, if you start with the right mindset, you will notice that changing into a better you isn't hard. For starters, you need to be nobody else but the old you. No one is born with a bad habit. They are learned. A child doesn't tell lies because speaking to them feels good. They do it because they have seen it help them get out of an otherwise bad situation. Through lying, they have awarded themselves an escape from punishment and thus are drawn to that behavior every time they find themselves in a rut.

If it was learned behavior, it means that it can be unlearned, too. You can break the chain of bad habits. You don't need to give up drinking; you just need to return to being a sober individual. You don't need to transform into a healthy person; you just need to return to eating healthy. If you recall, takeout meals weren't as common when we were young. We had home-cooked meals most of the day, right from the oven. We switched to takeout meals because they came easier and cheaper. There was no cooking or cleaning involved. It saved you time—time which you still wasted doing something equally unimportant. The point is, you lived without this habit when you were young. If you survived without it then, you can survive without it now as well. Think of it as going on a social media cleanse that has become a common norm among people these days.

This idea may work for you but not for a child. Their exposure and experience are different from yours. They will need more convincing on why they should give up something that is labeled bad for them, especially when it feels so good. They may take in all the factual information of why it isn't good, but what about when it comes to initiating a new habit?

To instill new habits, make sure that you break down the habit into smaller goals first. No one climbs a mountain the first time. You need to take small steps and gradually reach the desired peak. Instilling a new habit is a slow and steady process. You can't expect your children to rush through it. Breaking down the end goal into smaller, more achievable goals makes it easier to stay on track and remain motivated.

Furthermore, visualize yourself succeeding. See yourself breaking each cigarette or throwing away the box.

Visualize yourself buying healthy produce. If the goal is to lose weight, visualize waking up early, playing some rock songs, and going on a walk in the park. The more specific you are with the image in your mind, the more real it will become. Visualizing yourself crushing your goals with a smile on your face will help you make peace with the new habits you want to replace the old ones with.

Track your child's progress as well. Be sure to set a small reward for the achievement of every small goal. A little celebration will keep them encouraged. Tracking their progress will let them know how far they can come from where they started. That should give them a feeling of pride.

Chapter 6:

Active Listening and Empathy

In broken homes, where parents have split or are not on good terms, many things go unsaid and unheard. Children feel neglected and ignored because the parents don't know how to work as a team and raise children as happily as possible.

Being empathetic toward children, especially when they reach their teenage years, is important. They are going through so many physical and hormonal changes. They need guidance and support to understand all that is going on. An absent or disinterested parent, in this case, is of no use. They can't have healthy interactions with their children because they feel so engrossed in their issues, negatively impacting the atmosphere in the house.

Empathy is an act of showing support and kindness. It involves understanding another person's perspectives without judgment or criticism. It involves showing kindness and consideration. You must lend a shoulder to cry on as well as a present mind and ear. You must listen as well as decipher the words that remain unsaid.

For parents that live separately, this can be more challenging. However, if the intention is there, a strong bond will form. An intention to hear without offering unsolicited advice and a willingness to sit through and not pass comments or get distracted is a must. These are the two pillars of active listening.

Being available isn't enough. Your child should feel your genuine support and compassion for them. A simple pat on the back, an embrace, or a kiss on the forehead can be great strategies to help children feel better when distressed.

In this chapter, we talk about the importance of showing consideration and compassion toward children through active listening.

How Active Listening Strengthens Bonds

Family dynamics and interactions between family members improve when people feel heard. It makes them feel important and valued. Active listening is pivotal for all family types, whether nuclear, single, or co-parenting. It has many benefits. For parents, it means better comprehension of their children's feelings and emotions. This is a common complaint of parents living with one or more teenagers in the house. They feel isolated and disconnected. They speak about a lack of communication because there are always conflicting views and arguments happening. Parents are trying to model good behaviors by restricting children from certain activities and companies whereas children crave more independence and control over their lives.

Active listeners are better communicators. They don't only listen to what the person is saying but also notice their body language and facial expressions. They can sense when a person feels uncomfortable speaking about something awkward by noticing the changes in their tone. They tend to delay bringing up the topic or try to abstain from using certain words. Active listeners are also great problem-solvers. Since they can give someone their undivided attention, they can come up with solutions that aren't based on emotions like anger or frustration. It's like stopping your drunk friend from calling an ex because you know they are going to regret it later.

Becoming an active listener should be the goal of every parent. It is the easiest way to stay in touch and connected with your child—no matter what their age or where they are. Active listening cultivates an environment in the house where there are fewer misunderstandings. There is respect and acceptance for each other's feelings and emotions, and no one feels misunderstood or taken advantage of. It also fosters an ambiance where it becomes easier to have hard conversations about topics such as safe sex practices, different types of sexual harassment, emotional abuse, peer pressure, gender, racial discrimination, etc. Parents can be open about these topics and have healthy conversations as opposed to avoiding having these conversations.

Active listening also makes for a safe space for children who have few friends or are naturally shy. They can come to you with their problems and find solutions together as a team. Active listening skills can also help you set clear expectations from your children. When you listen to them carefully, you can identify the things that interest them and set expectations accordingly. By becoming an active listener, you can also give children more freedom. You can empower them to take on challenges self-reliantly. By supporting them in their fears and boosting their morale, you can better prepare them for the world that's out there.

Becoming an Active Listener

Overall, your bond with your child will be strengthened if they sense your support and backing. You don't have to agree with everything they share with you; you just have to validate that you hear and comprehend what they are saying.

You may feel like you aren't currently an effective listener because you feel disconnected from your child. You worry they will have to deal with all their problems alone without guidance and mentorship. However, the path to becoming an active listener is simple. There is an art to it, and it can be mastered. Below is a step-by-step module to make you a better listener for your partner as well as your child.

Be Attentive: Put down your phone, get away from what you were engaged in, and find yourself and your child in a distraction-free and comfortable space. Only then can you promise them all your attention and support.

Maintain Steady Eye Contact: Sometimes, when one person keeps speaking, the other tends to get distracted. They lose track of the thought, and their mind goes elsewhere. They also lose eye contact. Eye contact is an essential component of active listening. It makes you appear warm, approachable, and reliable. It makes the speaker more confident and active. It also allows you to read their facial expressions.

Ask Open-Ended Questions: Open-ended questions make for another excellent tip. Asking questions that require further clarification tells the speaker you are equally engaged in the conversation as they are. It shows them that you are genuinely interested in offering your support and consideration because you want to know more about their problem.

Avoid Interrupting Them: If the speaker is going with the flow or in a moment where their words are flowing like water, avoid interrupting them or making any noises that break that tempo. Let them go at their own pace without requesting them to speed up or slow down.

Request Clarification: In case you find an idea or emotion confusing, seek clarification. Probe the speaker to offer more insights for better comprehension.

Repeat Back: Repeating back what you have heard after the speaker has finished speaking makes them feel understood. You don't have to exactly say their sentences verbatim; you can add or remove words as per your liking. Ask them if you have it right or wrong. They will let you know and correct what you need.

Summarize: Finally, summarize what you have heard and let them know what you think. If the speaker seeks advice, offer it to them. If they just wanted to vent out their emotions, let them know that you are thankful for their thoughtfulness to consider you as a listener.

Chapter 7:

Scheduling Quality Time Together

It has become a need of today that both parents contribute financially to keep the house running. In many households, both parents have to work full time to pay the bills. In such homes, there is little room for spending quality time with the children. The burden is doubled in homes with single parents raising a child, or children, on their own.

Scheduling quality time with the children every day is crucial for their healthy development and growth. It is a time where parents can bond with their children and gain more insights about their lives, friends, school, etc. They can talk about important issues or discuss school-related progress. This free time dedicated to your children should be utilized in ensuring that they feel important and loved. They should know and feel grateful for the presence and support of their parents.

When it comes to spending quality time with your children, the first question that comes to one's mind is, "What defines quality?" Is there a tool to measure the success or failure of the time spent together? How can you know that your child enjoys and looks forward to this particular hour in the day? Quality time is dedicated time. If you have more than one child, it means giving each individual their undivided attention, doing things they love doing, or talking about stuff that interests them. For example, if your child is interested in sports, you can watch a game together; talk about team players and their strengths; or spend time creating your fantasy league team. Similarly, if your child is interested in playing music, you can build a small studio where you practice with them together and create new melodies.

Quality time means solely focusing on them. You put away your gadgets, turn off the TV, and listen to what they have to say. If they are doing homework, you help them with it. if they are playing a game, you join in. If they are finishing a puzzle, you set up the pieces for them. These are all examples of how you can make the most of your time together.

The goal is to bond and connect with your child so that they view you as more than a parent but also a friend. They should feel comfortable sharing things with you without the fear of being judged. They should be able to count on your support, insights, and wisdom. They should feel blessed to have someone that validates their emotions and feelings and helps cope with them.

Benefits of Family Downtime

In one study, researchers looked at how spending more time with children impacted their academics (Repetti et al., 2015). A mother's attention was the prime variant. After reviewing the evidence, it was found that a parent's attention and interest not only helped children excel in academics but also improved behavior and emotional well-being. The reason to mention this isn't to negate the importance of spending time with children but to reinforce that quality time is more important than its quantity. Giving children high-quality time which involves talking about the things that interest them is more beneficial than forcing them to do something they don't like. When children feel validated for who they are, their feelings toward their parents become positive. They begin to view them as their friends from just an authority figure. They become more drawn toward helping them out with the chores because they enjoy the time they spend with them.

This proves that quality time is more important than spending more time with children. In her blog, Catherine Jones talked about the most common behavioral issues in children at school and home. She then links it with the parent-child dynamic to further understand the environment at home. She found that children are less likely to misbehave or engage in risky behaviors when their parents spend quality time with them (Jones, 2017). There was a reduced risk of such children finding themselves in drugs and alcohol usage.

When you show your children that you love and support them, they don't have to look for the same attention elsewhere. Parents who spend quality time with their kids also raise physically healthier children (Anderson et al., 2011). The reason is good nutrition and a structured routine that contributes to good quality of sleep.

In short, spending quality downtime with the kids fosters a loving and affectionate environment. It cultivates harmony between the parents and children, making sure that healthy family dynamics prevail.

As for parents, they can learn to appreciate their children more when they come to know of their unique talents, personalities, and traits. When every child brings a unique set of skills and personalities to the mix, parents can appreciate the diversity in the house. They can connect better and feel comfortable discussing important issues that children must be made aware of while growing up.

Family Activities Ideas for Downtime

Quality time can lead to some amazing insights about each other. Attempting something new like building furniture, painting a wall, assembling a shelf, or playing games and doing activities together can make for some amazing memories and laughter, improving trust and connection between all parties.

Eating meals together is an activity that comes most recommended by experts. From preparing the meals to setting the table and eating it, it serves as a great opportunity for parents and children to bond together. They can help each other out, talk about how their day went, and discuss any events or school programs parents should know about.

Going grocery shopping is another fun way to spend quality time with children. Shopping can make for some amazing skill-building activities. One can learn about money management, etiquettes of standing in a line at a checkout, and read labels off the product to know about their nutritional benefits.

Bedtime stories also make for some amazing quality time. You can go book shopping with your children and have them pick books of their choosing. Then, you can set aside a time to read together and experience something magical.

Scheduling game nights where you play games like Monopoly, Scrabble, or Pictionary can also become the cause of laughter and happiness in the house. You can schedule one every weekend and have all your children gather in the lounge or living room to play. On some weekends, you can use the same time to DIY some arts and crafts or prepare a set of house rules that applies to everyone.

Finally, you can watch age-appropriate movies together and have a great discussion after the movie ends where you talk about character roles, story plots, and the choices made by that character. You can expose young children to a wide range of topics, cultures, as well as races so that they become more tolerant and appreciative of diversity.

Conclusion

Parenting is a team effort. Long gone are those days where women were supposed to look after the kids on their own while the men hunted for food in the wild. Today, the research looks at the benefits each parental figure brings into the life of a child, what role each of them plays, and how important it is to set aside time for family.

In this book, we looked at how, by working as a team, we can improve family dynamics in the house and provide our children with a prospering environment. We looked at how we can cultivate positive habits and replace bad ones through tact and determination. We talked about how families can improve lines of communication by becoming more open, supportive, and empathetic toward children. We studied the various factors that come into play like different communication styles, patterns, and areas. We then delved into the world of acknowledging common problems among families that ruin relational interactions and make them bitter. From tantrums to disrespect, we covered different aspects and looked at how these issues can be resolved within the house in a calm and structured manner.

In the final chapters, we then looked at how becoming an active listener and scheduling downtime with the kids improves their well-being and makes them happier. We talked about how we can schedule free time and the many activities we can engage in.

The goal of the book is to encourage parents to see parenting as an act of teamwork. It doesn't matter if you are raising a child on your own or accompanied by your ex-spouse, your priorities should be your children.

Thank you for giving this book a read. I hope you loved reading it as much as I enjoyed writing it. It would make me the happiest person on earth if you would take a moment to leave an honest review. All you have to do is visit the site where you purchased this book: It's that simple! The review doesn"t have to be a full-fledged paragraph; a few words will do. Your few words will help others decide if this is what they should be reading as well. Thank you in advance, and best of luck with your parenting adventures. Every moment is a joyous one with a child.

References

7 key active listening skills. (2020, April 1). The Cengage Blog. https://blog.cengage.com/7-key-active-listening-skills/

Anderson, S. E., Gooze, R. A., Lemeshow, S., & Whitaker, R. C. (2011). Quality of early maternal-child relationship and risk of adolescent obesity. PEDIATRICS, 129(1), 132–140. https://doi.org/10.1542/peds.2011-0972

Applebury, G. (n.d.). *Understanding family dynamics and their impact.* LoveToKnow. https://family.lovetoknow.com/about-family-values/understanding-family-dynamics-their-impact

B, N. (2019, October 26). *Understanding family dynamics meaning and family types.* TheMindFool. https://themindfool.com/understanding-family-dynamics-meaning-and-family-types/

Brown, A. (2017, December 27). *What is the importance of family in modern society?* Betterhelp.com; BetterHelp. https://www.betterhelp.com/advice/family/what-is-the-importance-of-family-in-modern-society/

Brown, A. (2021, November 19). *Growing share of childless adults in U.S. don't expect to ever have children*. Pew Research Center. https://www.pewresearch.org/fact-tank/2021/11/19/growing-share-of-childless-adults-in-u-s-dont-expect-to-ever-have-children/

Butler, C. (2020, April 13). *How to create healthy habits that strengthen your family (part 1)*. Quick and Dirty Tips. https://www.quickanddirtytips.com/parenting/school-age/10-healthy-habits-that-strengthen-your-family-part-1

Clear, J. (2013, May 13). *How to break a bad habit (and replace it with a good one)*. James Clear. https://jamesclear.com/how-to-break-a-bad-habit

Communication - family relationships. (n.d.). Family.jrank.org. Retrieved December 18, 2021, from https://family.jrank.org/pages/290/Communication-FAMILY-RELATIONSHIPS.html

DeFrain, J., & Asay, S. M. (2007). Strong families around the world. *Marriage & Family Review*, *41*(1-2), 1–10. https://doi.org/10.1300/j002v41n01_01

Duford, C. (2016, June 10). *5 ways to improve family relationships*. Intermountainhealthcare.org.

https://intermountainhealthcare.org/blogs/topics/heart/2016/06/5-ways-to-improve-family-relationships/

Duxbury, L., Stevenson, M., & Higgins, C. (2018). Too much to do, too little time: Role overload and stress in a multi-role environment. *International Journal of Stress Management*, *25*(3), 250–266. https://doi.org/10.1037/str0000062

Family dynamics - strong bonds - building family connections. (2019). Jss.org.au. http://www.strongbonds.jss.org.au/workers/families/dynamics.html

Important factors that contribute to healthy family dynamics. (2019, June 19). Www.originsrecovery.com. https://www.originsrecovery.com/family-dynamics/

Improve your child's active listening skills | oxford learning. (2017, July 27). Oxford Learning. https://www.oxfordlearning.com/improve-active-listening-skills/

Improving family communications. (2015, November 21). HealthyChildren.org. https://www.healthychildren.org/English/family-life/family-dynamics/communication-discipline/Pages/Improving-Family-Communications.aspx

Jones, C. (2017). What are the benefits of spending quality time with your kids. https://10minutesofqualitytime.com/what-are-the-benefits-spending-quality-time-kids/

Markman, H. J. (1981). Prediction of marital distress: A 5-year follow-up. *Journal of Consulting and Clinical Psychology*, *49*(5), 760–762. https://doi.org/10.1037/0022-006x.49.5.760

MedCircle. (2021, February 2). *Family dynamics: Attachment theory, communication, & relationships*. MedCircle. https://medcircle.com/articles/family-dynamics/

Miller, I. W., Ryan, C. E., Keitner, G. I., Bishop, D. S., & Epstein, N. B. (2000). The mcmaster approach to families: Theory, assessment, treatment and research. *Journal of Family Therapy*, *22*(2), 168–189. https://doi.org/10.1111/1467-6427.00145

Noller, P., & Fitzpatrick, M. A. (1990). Marital communication in the eighties. *Journal of Marriage and the Family*, *52*(4), 832. https://doi.org/10.2307/353305

Peterson, R. (2009, May 1). *Families first-keys to successful family functioning: Communication*. Vt.edu. https://www.pubs.ext.vt.edu/350/350-092/350-092.html

Repetti, R. L., Reynolds, B. M., & Sears, M. S. (2015). Families under the microscope: Repeated sampling of perceptions, experiences, biology, and behavior. Journal of Marriage and Family, 77(1), 126–146. https://doi.org/10.1111/jomf.12143

Slattengren, K. (n.d.). *Improving your family dynamics.* Www.pricelessparenting.com. Retrieved December 19, 2021, from https://www.pricelessparenting.com/documents/improving-your-family-dynamics

The 10 most common family problems and how to deal with them. (2020, February 7). IPC. https://theinternationalpsychologyclinic.com/the-10-most common-family-problems-and-how-to-deal-with-them/

Thomas, P. A., Liu, H., & Umberson, D. (2017). Family relationships and well-being. *Innovation in Aging, 1*(3), 1–11. https://doi.org/10.1093/geroni/igx025

Tolstoy, L. (1878). *Anna Karenina.* The Russian Messenger.

Zitzman, B. (2019, November 18). *Importance of family | why is family important [really important].* Family Today. https://www.familytoday.com/relationships/importance-of-family/

www.ingramcontent.com/pod-product-compliance
Lightning Source LLC
LaVergne TN
LVHW051019080826
845145LV00009B/2698

9781956018288